Nordic Walking:
A Total Body Experience
by Tim "T-Bone" Arem

© Copyright 2006, Tim Arem

Published by BookSurge Publishing

First Edition

Publisher's Cataloging-in-Publication Data

Arem, Tim (1952-   )
Nordic walking: A total body experience/by Tim Arem—1st ed.
p. cm.
SUMMARY: An introduction to the sport of Nordic walking, including a look at its many health benefits.

LCCN
ISBN   1-4196-4662-1

About the Author

Tim "T-Bone" Arem, M.Ed. author, Nordic walking instructor, America's Health and Fitness Ambassador, former Ronald McDonald, Mac Tonight, Donatello (Ninja Turtle), radio show host, school teacher, white water rafting guide, magician, professional clown, circus arts performer.

Carpe Diem
(seize the day)

Acknowledgments

Linda Speizer, for her stewardship in introducing me to Nordic walking and for being the ultimate "Pole Goddess".

Suzanne Nottingham, for her insightful thoughts, comments, and suggestions.

Jennifer Sawyer, for her computer skills and personality.

Sawako Jager, for her invaluable assistance, suggestions, and sustenance during the research and writing of this book.

Tom Rutlin, for being an awesome ambassador of Nordic walking.

The Arem Clan, for their belief in me.

Graham Watts, for providing outstanding photographs and support.

Dan Barrett, for spreading Nordic walking to the fitness community.

Pete Edwards, for being an outstanding ambassador of Nordic walking, "ski walking" and an informative instructor and teacher.

Greg Wozer, for having the vision of sharing Nordic walking as the activity continues to grow in the Western Hemisphere.

Jeanne Goldberg, for ageless inspiration and energy.

Gottfied Kuermer, for being the ultimate Master Trainer and teacher. Many thanks for setting the standard so high.

Gene Verel: for giving me my first Nordic walking class.

The Florida core group, for being the unique individuals that helped make our training so outstanding.

Mike Crisp, for fun illustrations.

Scott Smith, for his vision and creativity.

Frank Forrester, for great photos.

Nate "The Wing Man" Goldberg, for his mentoring and great ideas on working with active adults.

Jack Affleck, for his awesome pictures of Beaver Creek Resort.

Introduction

I expect that the book you now hold in you hands is the first one you have seen on the subject of Nordic walking. In this day of the Internet, there is a ton of information with more than 6 million references on Nordic walking (e.g. Google "Nordic walking".) Then "why?" you ask, "create a book?" The reason I decided to write about this subject is because I wanted to have one easy-to-read source for people to use.

This activity is so relatively new in this country that I wanted to be able to share it with the masses. I've been speaking to groups whenever possible, but I can only tell so many people by word-of-mouth.

The benefits of Nordic walking are amazing. There are many former athletes and people recovering from past sport injuries where perhaps people overextended themselves and are looking for a total body activity that everyone, regardless of athletic ability, can enjoy and benefit from.

I'd like people to read this book who are willing to accept new ideas and have a willingness to share their findings with others. Nordic walking is for both the young and the young at heart, for people from all walks of life, and for all athletic levels.

Few can keep up with the thousands of articles published each month about Nordic walking. This book will help you make sense of this voluminous information and more importantly, show you how to use it to improve your own life.

Ten most common things a Nordic Walker is likely to hear:
- Are we expecting snow?
- Do the poles go in front or in back of my body?
- Did you forget your skis?
- Do you really need two poles?
- Where do you get those sticks?
- Are those feet on the end of those things?
- Why can't I use my trekking poles to go Nordic walking?
- Do you really get a workout with those?
- Can these poles be used to fend off critters?
- These poles are so light! Shouldn't they be heavier in order for me to get a real workout?

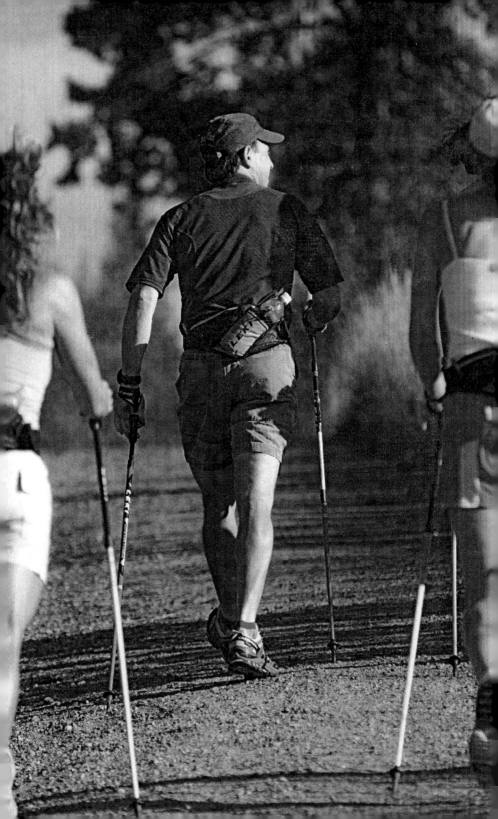

Chapter One

"If at first, the idea is not absurd,
then there is no hope for it."
~ Albert Einstein

History

"Where's the snow?" This was the first comment I heard on a weekend stroll in downtown Asheville, North Carolina while Nordic walking. *Excel*, a pole manufacturer and the first commercial company to bring their Nordic walking poles to the market, define Nordic walking as "Fitness walking with specifically designed poles." As with new innovations in our history, people wonder what Nordic walking is and why we do it.

The Wright Brothers must have had a heck of a time at Kitty Hawk explaining their "flying machine" to the onlookers. And I can't imagine being in the crowd for the launch in Paris for Barol Karl Dravis von Sauerboon's "two-wheel cycle," the creation we now call the bicycle.

With Nordic walking, seeing and experiencing is believing. When I've explained in person (without my Nordic walking poles) and on the phone what Nordic walking is, some people think I have lost my marbles. "Why would you want to walk with poles?" That's another popular response. To get a grasp of what Nordic walking is and where its roots developed, my research took me to Scandinavia.

It's believed that it started in the 1930s during the off-season from cross-country skiing. The walking-with-pole activity was used as a summer training program to stay in competitive form. The majority of sources mention that Nordic walking experienced a rebirth in popularity in the late 1990s in Finland where presently 760,000 walkers maintain the activity as part of their weekly lifestyle.

Nordic walking has since spread to Germany, Australia, New Zealand, parts of Europe, Canada, and finally to the United States. Another school of thought with regards to history has come across my desk from several sources.

Tom Rutlin, an early Nordic walking enthusiast and trainer in the Unites States whose name is often overlooked in the sport's history, has an interesting story. Besides having a comprehensive website (see "Cool Websites"), Mr. Rutlin appears to have been on the ground floor of the Nordic walking movement. In his open letter in 1988 to the Nordic walking community, he founded Exerstrider which he defined as a concept of using specifically designed poles as a form of regular exercise. His pioneer work in this field, putting rubber feet on poles and walking, places his concept a decade ahead of the big manufacturers. Rutlin appears to be a forward thinking individual who rightly deserves credit. In his own words:

"What most people really need and want is simply to put their entire body to 'good use' so that they can begin functioning at a higher level, feel good, have vitality, and live long active lives." That is exactly what Nordic walking is all about.

As with many trends and activities that have begun outside the United States, Nordic walking is relatively new to Americans and has taken some time to become part of our culture. Nordic walkers, however, are now being spotted in pockets throughout the United Sates, from Oregon to Florida.

The growth and future of this social activity lies in word-of-mouth "advertising" and the development of Nordic walking communities. As with most things unique and different, the more people see and experience Nordic walking, the larger the growth will occur. On a personal level, the Nordic walking club I started in Asheville is enjoying consistent growth as more members talk about it and others see us in action seemingly looking for snow in the summertime!

Nordic walking is here to stay. I say that because it is most definitely not a fitness craze that will come and go overnight. More and more folks are discovering that Nordic walking is one of the most beneficial types of exercise — benefits that are discussed in the next chapter.

So how many of us are there? The estimated population of Nordic walkers at the end of 2005 worldwide was 7 million and growing.

7 Million and Growing

"My neighbor asked me what I was doing, that my posture has improved? I told her I was Nordic walking"
~ Givens Estates Retirement Community Resident, Asheville, N.C.

Chapter Two

"We are what we repeatedly do;
excellence, then, is not an act but a habit."
~ Aristotle

Benefits

The research is in and the doctors have spoken. Nordic walking is one of the most effective of the low impact cardiovascular exercises. This activity works with more muscle groups in the body and offers more health benefits than regular walking, jogging, biking, or swimming.

Recent studies by the Dallas-based Cooper Institute (an organization that works to promote a wider understanding of the relationship between lifestyles and health)indicate that Nordic walking burns more calories, more greatly increases oxygen consumption, and can be up to 46% more efficient than normal walking. (This would account for the increase in weight loss and lowering of cholesterol experienced by many Nordic walkers.) Normal walking uses approximately 70% of the muscle mass in the body at any given time. While using the proper Nordic walking technique, that muscle mass percentage rises to 90%.

Have you ever experienced an enhanced mood after exercising? This is called a runner's high and is caused by the release of endorphins in the body. The same enhanced mood occurs with Nordic walking.

When I Nordic walk, I'm able to focus on myself rather than the events of the day. My friend Jeanne Goldenburg has done a great deal of research on anti-aging. Her belief is that Nordic walking is a very effective activity for the brain. She suggests two inspiring books: *The Better Brain Book* by David Perlmutter, M.D. (www.betterbrainbook.com) and *Fantastic Voyage* by Ray Kurzweil and Terry Grossman, M.D. Both these texts focus on brain fitness. We often talk about exercising our bodies, perhaps we should spend more time and energy on our brains, too.

Two of the ancillary benefits you get from walking with the poles are balance and stability. I had one woman say to me that she can finally walk by herself and not depend on her husband's arm. In fact, we have several folks walk with us while using their Nordic walking poles rather than their walkers!

The upper body also benefits when we participate in Nordic walking, by improving neck and chest mobility. Neck and shoulder pain has a higher likelihood of being relieved with Nordic walking rather than normal walking.

One of the really neat things about walking with the poles is that it provides more exercise with less perceived exertion, and thus we are more likely to keep it up. This activity helps to lower your resting heart rate. With the poles, more ground is covered in a shorter amount of time.

This exercise strengthens the upper body and back muscles. There has been a lot of research and information on osteoporosis. Nordic walking strengthens bones and reinforces an upright posture by virtue of proper pole placement. With continued walking, bone health increases. This activity is easy on the joints and knees. The lower body along with the upper body gets a total body workout with Nordic walking.

Active adults from Givens Estate Retirement Community Asheville, NC

This social fitness activity encourages a positive trans- formation of the body from the inside out by improving several of the body systems — skeletal, mus- cular, immune, cardiovascular, and my personal favorite, the feeling good system, Okay, the last one isn't really a system. But when you feel good on the inside, chances are your outside will look and feel good, too.

Chapter Three

*"Progress always involves risk; you can't steal
second base and keep your feet on first."*
~ *Frederick Wilcox*

Equipment

The most important gear for Nordic walking consists of walking
shoes and poles. Let's focus on the shoes and discuss poles later in
this book.

Walking Shoes — Look for shoes with maximum comfort. The
walking and running shoe industry has grown by leaps and bounds

since the days in the 1960s when all I'd wear were my Keds. Specialty stores are extremely popular now and salespeople tend to be very knowledgeable. Quite often, the employees tend to be runners and walkers themselves and are knowledgeable people with a major focus on customer service and satisfaction.

There is a growing debate on the use of running shoes for walking. Running shoes have more of a history, and the technology for both types of shoes have come a long way. But there are differences. Running requires more cushioning and stability than walking. Therefore, the soles on running shoes tend to be thicker. Overall, there are more choices to choose from than there are with walking shoes.

Walking shoes differ in that they are specifically designed to help propel you through the heel-toe motion. Runners tend to land flat-footed, rather than on their heels as walkers do. The manufacturers are well aware of this and have made the heels of walking shoes beveled to increase stability. I recommend walking shoes for serious walkers. Many of the folks I see on the Nordic walks in the urban setting have been using either one. I've included both running and walking websites in the book.

It's best to have an understanding of some shoe terms prior to going to the store. Most people's feet fall into three different foot types: pronators, supinators, and neutral feet.

An easy way to figure your foot type is to take a pair of shoes you have worn for a while and put them on the table. Stand behind them and look. If the shoes cave inward, you are most likely a pronator (this is the most common type of foot). Conversely, if they cave outward, chances are you're a supinator. A neutral foot would show slight signs of caving. When shopping, take a pair of well-worn shoes to show the salesperson. They will know by looking at the shoes what foot type you have.

Here are some tips for shopping for a walking shoe. Go at the end of the day when your dogs (feet) are at the maximum size for the day, and wear the socks you walk in. Socks vary in thickness and you may have to adjust the size of the shoe. As we get older, our feet flatten out, so be sure to get them measured. One of the worst things you can do is to purchase a pair of shoes that are too small.

With your shoes on, make sure you have a finger's width from your big toe to the end of the shoe. Walk around the store/mall/ neighborhood to test the shoes. Your new investment in fitness needs to be comfortable. Look for shoes with removable insoles, good stability, cushioning, and shock absorbency. Last but not least, have fun with the experience.

Socks — As with shoes, manufacturers have made huge advances in style, texture, materials, comfort, and color of socks. To help prevent blisters, chaffing, and athlete's foot, wear socks. Unless you are creating a fashion movement and have a fondness for stinky shoes, wearing socks has many advantages. Good socks and shoes will add that one-two punch to your Nordic walking experience.

How will you know what brand and style of sock to choose? Good question. Similar to shoe, a little education will help. The choices of socks vary from cotton to synthetic. I wouldn't suggest tube socks (like the kind I mistakenly wore during my high school basketball career). Tube socks have three things going for them. First, they're cheap (Dad loved that). Second, they bunch up around my toes and third, they quickly lose their shape.

I've had success with synthetic socks. They wick away sweat from the feet, dry quickly, and retain their shape. Try on various brands before you purchase. If your socks have holes or you have worn them since the ice age, give them the heave-ho and treat your feet to some new and comfortable socks. Some of the most popular brands are Thorlo, Smart Wool, Wigwam, and Defeet (see the website section of this book for more information).

Poles, Poles Everywhere — Which Nordic walking poles are the right ones for you? As with shoes and socks, each person has a personal choice. In my research, I've located 13 companies that manufacture poles. Several things to consider before purchasing a set of poles:
- Has the company been in existence for a while?
- What kind of warranty comes with the poles? (A warranty generally comes on the metal shaft. For comparison the LEKI poles have a lifetime warranty on the poles.)
- Can I try different types of poles at my local retailer? (The only problem might be if the local

outdoor store carries only one
or two brands.)

- Does the pole company sponsor
local clinics at their retail stores?

Getting the right length is important.
To get the proper length according to
your height, this chart can help
(I've also included an illustration to help guide
you on page 14).

Height	Approx. Pole Size (cm)
4'9" – 4'11"	100
5'0" – 5'2"	105
5'3" – 5'5"	110
5'6" – 5'8"	115
5'9" – 5'10"	120
5'11" – 6'1"	125
6'2" – 6'4"	130
6'5" – 6'7"	135
6'8" – 6'10"	140

To properly adjust the length of the poles, begin with one pole first.
Start by holding one of the poles horizontally in your right hand.
Loosen the pole with your other hand by twisting the pole away from
you until you can slide the sections of the pole in and out. Extend the
pole to its full length. Note: Some poles have words such as
"Stop" or "Max" to let you know how far you can extend them.

Hold the pole vertically in your right hand so that the lower tip is out a bit to the side of your right foot. Tap the pole gently against the ground to shorten the pole slightly. Stand with your right elbow bent at appoximately a 90-degree angle and tighten the pole. Measure the second pole against the first and adjust it to be the same length. (See illustration to the left.)

That's it. Now You're set to go!

Some questions about poles —

- Does going online offer more choices? *(Answer: I prefer getting poles that I can try out in a store versus an online purchase.)*
- What is my budget?
- Can good poles really be purchased for under $30? *(Answer: The better poles will run you about $100.)*
- Will the retail staff at an outdoor store really know how to size the poles? *(Answer: They are getting better at this.)*
- Should I get poles with especially designed straps or will a wrist loop do? *(Answer: Go for the designed straps. The straps need to feel comfortable. I suggest the trigger or*

Velcro™. You want your hand to be snug with the pole. Leave the Vulcan death grip to Star Trek. The grip helps transfer your hand "force" to the poles.)

- Does it matter if the grip is made of cork, plastic, or synthetic foam? *(Answer: Personal preference holds the key here.)*
- Does it make a difference what material is used to make the shaft? *(Answer: Carbon/fiberglass composites, carbon, or aluminum poles are the most popular choices. If you walk often, you may want a higher end pole for lightness. Aluminum tends to be heavier than composites or carbon.)*
- Should I take classes with a trained instructor? *(Answer: A good idea. That way, you can make certain you're using the right techniques and getting the maximum benefit.)*
- Should I get adjustable or non-adjustable poles? *(Answer: Good question! The adjustable poles have several advantages: one size fits more than one person, and the length can vary for different terrain and workouts. An example of this is going up or down hills. When traveling by air, it's nice to be able to pack the pole in your cargo luggage. Poles are no longer allowed as part of your carry-on luggage. Disadvantages are that the locking mechanism needs to be checked for tightness —especially important for older folks. Also, there tends to be more vibration with adjustable than with non-adjustable poles.)*
- Are most of the tips the same for the poles? *(Answer: Yes, the standard is carbon tips. Concave tips help to grip a surface better than flat tips. Make sure you get the rubber feet or boots to put on the tips for indoor surfaces. My mall walkers love the little rubber feet. I prefer using the carbon tips and not the*

boots when I walk. It's a little noisier, but I like the grip I get. Walk with and without the rubber boots that fit snugly on the tips to get a feel of preference. A note to remember: have the rubber boots facing backward when you walk with the raised or heel facing your heel.)

It's a good idea to have as much reflective gear on as possible when you walk. Some pole companies make reflective straps and stickers for the poles.

To review, choose the poles that work best for you.

The pole purchase is an investment in your health; don't shortchange yourself.

Givens Estate Retirement Community Asheville, NC

Chapter Four

"Those who say it cannot be done should not interrupt those doing it."

~ *Unknown*

Warming Up, Cooling Down and Stretching

Warm-up and cool-down are two parts of Nordic walking that are too often ignored, especially by people on a tight fitness schedule. Take the time to do it right.

The rule of thumb is to give your body 5-10 minutes to warm up before you start the Nordic walk. Increasing the blood flow into the muscles will allow more freedom of movement help prevent injury. Your body temperature will rise as you do the warm-up. I like to tell the children I do assemblies for that the warm-up also is good for brain fitness. It gives your brain a chance to get in gear with your body. With the senior citizens with whom we work, the warm-up is simply walking in place with the poles held in a vertical stationary position along the side of the body. The main focus of the warm-up is the lower body. With our mind and body ready, we are ready to start the Nordic walk.

Nordic walking: A Total Body Experience

A big misconception in doing a workout is that you must first spend time stretching. I think this was taught in the PE (physical education) classes years ago. In my high school track workouts, however, the coach always had us run a slow mile before the stretching. We thought he was off his rocker. But as he explained it, our bodies needed to be "greased" before we did anything else. He also led us in yoga and had us do a number of sun salutations. It took me some time to realize that he was ahead of his time (this was the 1970s, after all). His track program was uniquely fun.

After we've finished our Nordic walk, what do we do now? A cool-down you say? That's correct. By the way, if you are in a group and you decide to stop, don't just stand around — do some light stretching. Save the games in Chapter 7 for after the cool-down. The word on the street for the cool-down, including the latest information from the American College of Sports Medicine, is to spend 5-10 minutes on this. The beginners should try for 10 minutes. This activity allows the body to shift back to normal. This is also an awesome time to think about what you just did for your walk and how you felt along the way.

The temperature of your body will also cool down at this time as your blood flows form you muscles back to the rest of your body. At this point in your workout, your muscles are ready for stretching. They are warm and tend to be more flexible. Let's not underestimate the importance of stretching for increased flexibility. Having a stretching routine after Nordic walking will benefit your total body from balance to posture and allow you to move more freely and comfortably. Having a full range of motion is a good thing.

Quad Stretch

- Stand tall with feet hip-width apart.

- Hold pole for support in front of you.

- Bend left leg with heel moving toward buttocks.

- Grasp foot gently with right hand.

- Relax the knee of base leg (don't lock.)

- Relax shoulders.

- Hold for 15-20 seconds.

- Switch to other leg.

- Repeat two times

Hamstring Stretch

- Plant both poles shoulder width apart.

- Lean back almost in a sitting position.

- Extend left foot so foot is in a vertical position against the pole.

- Hold for 15-20 seconds.

- Switch feet.

- Repeat two times.

Tricep Stretch

- Grab the top of the pole with one hand.

- Place pole over the head and straight down the middle of your back.

- Reach your other hand around the pole further down the shaft.

- Gently pull down with the lower hand to complete the stretch.

- Hold for 5-10 seconds.

- Switch hand positions.

- Repeat 2 times

Side Stretch

- Gently place pole on shoulders behind your neck.

- Hold overhand at both ends.

- Slowly twist body in one direction.

- Hold for 5-10 seconds.

- Twist to other side.

- Repeat 2 times.

Torso Stretch

- With arms extended grab one pole and hold horizontally at the ends.

- Stand with straight posture. Bend to side by shifting hips in opposite direction.

- Breathe out as you bend.

- Hold for 5-10 seconds.

- While breathing in through the nose come back to center position.

- Proceed to other side while breathing out and shifting opposite hips.

- Repeat 2 times.

Squat Stretch

- Grab both poles in a horizontal over-hand position in the center.

- Slightly bend your knees.

- Hold for 5-10 seconds.

- Repeat 2 times.

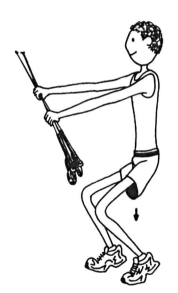

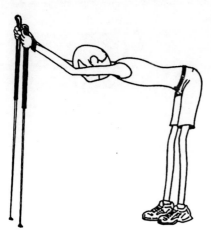

Back Stretch

- Place poles in front of you.

- With straight arms place weight on poles by leaning on them.

- Focus on bending from the waist.

Hip Stretch

- Hold both poles parallel in front.

- Bend arms slightly.

- Place right leg between both poles and bend.

- Outstretch the back leg.

- Keep back straight.

- Hold for 5-10 seconds.

- Switch position of your feet.

- Repeat 2 times.

Chapter Five

*"Start by doing what's necessary; then do what's possible;
and suddenly you are doing the impossible."*

~ Unknown

Technique

Ready, Set, Let's go Nordic walking — Basically the technique is very much like walking, however, your stride will be longer than normal with the use of the poles. The ends of the poles (the tips) stay behind while the arms swing in a close to normal walking pattern. Some important points to remember: Chin-up, not looking at your feet, shoulders stay relaxed, posture upright, and hands and feet work opposite of each other. To help you get started, here are four easy progressive steps to follow.

Before we start the steps, however, you have to find a flat level surface. A deserted parking lot is ideal, and so are a field, a sidewalk, and a nice ocean. Okay, just kidding about the ocean. Here's the moment you've been waiting for. You have the gear, you have the poles.

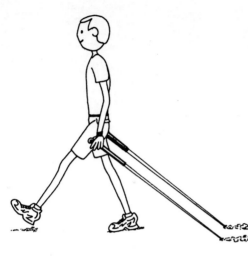

Step 1

After the poles have been measured to you and with your hands in the straps, your palms should be open and your arms relaxed by your sides. Now you're ready to walk about a hundred feet. I know this may look pretty simple, but humor me. This really gets your total body familiar with the poles. Nice job. Step 1 is complete.

Step 2

Begin by walking about 20 feet. After 20 feet, continue walking and gradually include your normal arm swing. This rhythm should be very similar to your normal walk. Go for 100 feet with the arm swing

added. So far so good...right? A helpful hint is to keep your arms long as you swing them. This swinging motion comes from the shoulder not the elbow. The poles are still dragging behind you.

Step 3

A quick review on form chin level, posture straight and shoulders relaxed.Now that you have mastered steps 1 and 2, proceed to the head of the class. If you have not caught on, then no dessert for a week. Seriously, if you're not in a comfortable rhythm after the hundred feet, start over with the first step and then add the arm swing again. For Step 3, gently grip the poles and start dragging them for a few feet or so, and then add the arm swing (you're doing great!). When you're ready, place the poles on the ground and apply a little force on the handle, especially on the back swing. This force will help propel you in a forward direction. At this point, the straps on the poles will guide the force to the poles.

I know this sounds like Star Wars (use the force, Luke...). Only a gentle force is used at this point. Another hundred feet or maybe once around the block is a nice walk for this step. At this time, folks generally don't want to stop because they are in a groove.

A hint here: if you're too winded or breathing to hard that you're not able to have a conversation while walking, slow your pace down. Later on, you can always speed up. Who was it that said the tortoise always beats the hare?

A quick review on form. Head up, eyes looking forward, shoulders relaxed, hands holding the grip lightly, and last but not least, make sure you're having a brilliant time.

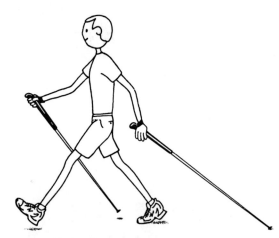

Step 4

Congratulations! You are now a Nordic walking machine. On to the final step. Step 4 is a piece of cake or pie. Continue with step 3 for a few feet. Now instead of dragging the poles, feel free to lift them as you place them. At this point, it's important to remember that the lead pole doesn't go ahead of the other foot's heel. By this time, you have the hang of all the steps and can call your self a Nordic walker. Continue walking on flat surfaces when you walk with the poles. As you get more daring in the weeks ahead, explore other types of terrain. Remember to keep safety first and have an awesome time.

> *Tip: On the back arm swing, open your hand to release the energy at the end of the swinging motion (see illustration).*

How often should you walk? According to the Surgeon General, you should exercise for 20-30 minutes 3-5 times a week. I also read recently that we should exercise 60 minutes per day and twice on Sunday! Well, I think you can take Sunday off as your day of rest. Remember, 30 minutes of Nordic walking is equivalent to 50 minutes of regular walking.

This might be a good place to remind you that with this low impact activity, you'll only get out of it what you put into it. And age makes very little difference. What I mean by this is that an active adult will reap incredible benefits just as much as a young adult. The important thing is that the physical well-being of both will be greatly enhanced with this outstanding social fitness activity.

Remember, the longer you do Nordic walking, the greater the benefits. This is an activity for life, not just a six-week class. These benefits include posture alignment, posture awareness and heart health. Now who would not want all that in their life?

"My husband doesn't puff (breathe heavily) anymore since he started using the poles." ~ Lee

Chapter Six

*"Every time you are tempted to react in the
same old way, ask if you want to be a prisoner
of the past or a pioneer of the future."*
~ *Deepak Chopra*

Healthy Recipes

Snacks and Hydration for the Road — Depending on the length of
your Nordic walk, it's a good idea to take along a snack and some
type of drink for hydration. I've included nine healthy snacks that
can be made easily at home. These fast and fit recipes can be
prepared prior to your walk. If you just want to buy energy bars,
I've included a list of the most popular *(see the back of this book in
the website section)*.

It's important to maintain hydration during your walk. Water and
hydration drinks really come in handy and can be vital to overall
well-being. The rule of thumb is to drink 6-8 ounces for every
15 minutes of walking. As our bodies can only absorb a small
amount of liquid at a time, it's important that your liquid intake be
consumed slowly over a period of time.

Apricot, Date and Nut Bars – *www.foodfit.com*

Recipe makes 15 bars

Ingredients:

⅓ cup dates, pitted and chopped

⅓ cup dried apricots, chopped

¾ cup flour

⅓ cup golden raisins

1 cup pecans, chopped

3 eggs

1½ cups firmly packed brown sugar

¾ teaspoon baking powder

¼ teaspoon salt

Instructions:

Preheat the oven to 350 degrees F and spray a 10-inch by 10-inch pan with non-stick spray. Toss the dates and apricots with 1 tablespoon of flour. Add the raisins and nuts and set aside. Place the eggs in a mixing bowl and whip them with an electric mixer until frothy. Gradually add the brown sugar and continue whipping until the mixture is thick (takes about 5 minutes). Combine the flour, baking powder, and salt in a separate bowl and fold it into the egg mixture. Next, fold in fruit and nut mixture. Spread the batter into the prepared pan and bake until golden brown and springy to the touch (about 20 minutes). When cool, cut into bars and store in an airtight container. They'll keep for up to 5 days.

Hearty and Healthy Energy Bar – *www.chetday.com*

Ingredients:

1 cup dried apricots

1 cup dried figs

1 cup dates

½ cup raisins

1 cup unsweetened coconut

½ cup almond butter

½ cup honey

Instructions:

Using a food processor, grind each of the following separately: apricots, figs, dates, and raisins. Add the unsweetened coconut. Mix together the almond butter and honey. Combine the fruit mixture and almond butter mixture. Form into bars or balls and chill in the refrigerator.

Healthy Energy Bars

Ingredients:

4 cups puffed whole grain cereal (wheat, rice or Kashi)

½ cup chopped walnuts

½ cup chopped pecans

½ cup slivered almonds

¼ cup sunflower seeds

2 tablespoons flaxseed (grind in coffee mill)

2 tablespoons wheat germ

2 tablespoons whey protein powder

Instructions:

Place ingredients in a large bowl and mix together:

In small pan, boil together:

⅓ cup peanut butter (chunky or natural)

⅓ cup honey

⅓ cup light corn syrup

Try different flavors by adding instead of corn syrup try fat-free caramel sauce (I love this one), or maple syrup. Bring all the ingredients to a boil and boil while stirring for a few minutes until mixture thickens.

Pour over dry ingredients and stir to mix well. Prepare cookie sheet with foil or parchment paper and press the mixture firmly into the pan. I have used both a rolling pin and a glass to pack the mixture into pan. Bake at 350 degrees F for 10-15 minutes. I suggest using top rack as this syrup could burn easily. Cool in pan and then invert on paper and remove baking foil or parchment paper. You may cut your bars in desired shape. Store bars in bags or plastic containers. Shorter baking time leaves bars chewy (with longer time they become crisp). Give this a try! What have you got to lose? Who know, you just might feel better and finish that 18-hole course with plenty of energy to spare.

I found a good place to order ingredients for this recipe online at www.bulkfoods.com, as they give good service and speedy shipping. Their prices are very good on bulk orders from 1 to 50 pounds.

(Letta Meinen's From Kitchen Magic – Including Tips, Hints and Tricks, available from www.booklocker.com)

Healthy Breakfast Energy Bars – *www.recipezarr.com*

Recipe makes 8-10 bars

Homemade breakfast bars full of goodness. Of course, you can vary the fruit, chocolate chips, etc. that you add.

Ingredients:

2 cups rolled oats (you can
   use flavored oats)

½ cup whole wheat flour

½ cup shredded coconut

½ cup chopped nuts
   (of your choice)

½ cup chocolate chips or
   dried fruit

½ cup honey

80 g low fat margarine

1 egg, lightly beaten

Instructions:

Mix oats, flour, coconut, nuts, and chocolate chips or fruit together in a bowl. Heat honey and low-fat margarine together in a saucepan or in the microwave until spread is melted and mixture combines when stirred. Allow to cool slightly and then whisk in egg. Pour liquid into dry ingredients and mix well. Line tray with baking paper and spread mixture out to about 2cm. Bake at 350 degrees F for 25 minutes.Cut into 8-10 pieces while still warm, then transfer to airtight container to store.

Homemade Energy Bars – *The National Peanut Board,*
www.nationalpeanutboard.com

If you are tired of eating yet another highly processed and
engineered food, give these prize-winning energy bars a chance.
They are easy to make, less expensive than commercial energy
bars (they cost only 25 cents per bar, or $4 for the entire recipe),
and they taste yummy.

Ingredients:

½ cup salted, dry-roasted peanuts

½ cup raisins, Craisins® (sweetened, dried cranberries) or
other dried fruit

½ cup roasted sunflower seed kernels

2 cups raw oatmeal, quick or old-fashioned

2 cups toasted rice cereal, such as Rice Krispies®

½ cup peanut butter (either crunchy or creamy)

½ cup packed brown sugar

½ cup light corn syrup

1 teaspoon vanilla

Instructions:

In a large bowl, mix together the peanuts, raisins, sunflower
seed kernels, oatmeal, and toasted rice cereal. Set aside. In a
medium microwavable bowl, combine the peanut butter, brown
sugar, and corn syrup. Microwave on high for 2 minutes. Add
vanilla and stir until blended. Pour the peanut butter mixture over
the dry ingredients and stir until coated. Spoon it onto an oiled
9x13 pan. Press down firmly (it helps to coat your fingers with
margarine, oil, or cooking spray). Let stand for an hour to harden,
then cut into 16 bars.

Almond Maple Granola – *CD Kitchen: www.cdkitchen.com*

Recipe makes 16 bars

Ingredients:

4 cups mixed organic whole grain flakes, such as oat, Kamut®, barley, and wheat

1 cup sliced natural almonds

2 tablespoons cold unsalted butter, cut into 6 pieces

¼ cup all-purpose flour

2 tablespoons sugar

1 inch salt

⅓ cup pure maple syrup

1 teaspoon pure vanilla extract

½ teaspoon pure almond extract

½ cup golden raisins

½ cup dried cranberries

Instructions:

Preheat the oven to 350 degrees F. Combine the whole grain flakes with the almonds on a large rimmed baking sheet. Spread in an even layer and toast for about 10 minutes, stirring once, until light golden. Transfer the grain mixture to a large bowl. Leave the oven on. Coat the warm baking sheet with 1 tablespoon of the butter.

In a mini processor, combine the remaining 1 tablespoon of butter with the flour, sugar, and salt and pulse until the mixture resembles course crumbs. Or you can pinch the ingredients together with your fingers. Add the crumbs to the grain mixture and toss. In a small pitcher, combine the maple syrup with the vanilla and almond extracts. Pour over the grain mixture and stir until the grains are evenly moistened.

Next, spread the granola on the buttered baking sheet in an even layer and toast for 12 to 14 minutes, stirring once, until golden and dry. Let cook completely then stir in the raisins and cranberries. (courtesy of CD Kitchen: www.cdkitchen.com)

Trail Mix Bars – *Simon and modified by www.food.kaboose.com*

Ingredients:

1 cup unsalted butter

¾ cup honey

1 teaspoon lemon juice

2 cups whole-wheat flour

1 cup quick cooking oats

½ cup wheat germ

2 eggs

¼ cup honey

1 cup chopped almonds

1 cup jumbo semisweet chocolate chips

½ cup chopped dates

½ cup chopped dried apricots

½ cup unsweetened flaked coconut

1 tablespoon sesame seeds

Instructions:

Preheat oven to 350 degrees F. In a medium bowl, mix together the butter, the 3/4 cup of honey, and lemon juice until well blended.

Combine the flour, oats, and wheat germ mix into the honey mixture. Spread evenly into the bottom of an ungreased 9x13 inch-baking pan. Set aside.

In another bowl, beat eggs while gradually pouring in 1/4 cup honey. Stir in almonds, chocolate chips, date, apricots, coconut, and sesame seeds until they are evenly distributed and well located. Spread over the crust in pan.

Bake for 30 to 35 minutes in the preheated oven or until center is set, and the top is lightly browned. Cool completely before cutting into bars.

Happy Trail Mix – *www.foodfit.com*
   Ingredients:
   1 cup low-fat granola
   ½ cup raisins
   ½ cup dried apricots
   ¼ cup roasted and salted almonds
   ¼ cup M&M's or other chocolate candies

Instructions:
Combine all of the ingredients in a mixing bowl. Store in an airtight container for up to 4 weeks.

Healthy Trail Mix – *eDiets.com — www.mealsmatter.org*

Most prepackaged trail mixes are loaded with sodium and hidden sugars. Not this recipe though! Good for your heart and friendly to your taste buds, this trail mix is a winner and one you don't have to feel guilty about snacking on. Make a large batch, seal in individual ziplock plastic bags and you'll have ready-to-eat, good-for-you snacks you can feel good about.

Ingredients:

¾ oz unsalted pretzels

1 tablespoon walnuts

1 tablespoon sliced almonds

⅓ tablespoon raisins

Instructions:

Combine pretzels, raisins, walnuts, and almonds. Serve and eat. It doesn't get any easier than that!

"My husband and I can finally walk together at the same pace. When I use the poles, I can keep up with him and it's less effort."   ~ Gracie

Chapter Seven

"We don't stop playing because we grow older,
we grow older because we stop playing."

~ Nana (Age 103)

Every Body Limbo!

Family and Group Icebreakers and Games:

I am a big believer in families taking the time to do activities together. Whether preparing a meal as a group activity or sitting down at the dinner table and breaking bread together, we need more family time in our communities.

I have included this section on family and group activities in a book about Nordic walking as a fun way to spend some quality time together. Icebreakers and games can be used before, during, or after a Nordic walk. When I am leading a new group of people who don't know each other, games like these are a wonderful way to break the ice. Nonthreatening games allow people to become more comfortable with each other.

Some of the games will have a familiar ring to them, having have been passed down from generation to generation, while others have an interesting twist because of using Nordic poles.

Pole Pass

The first on our list is the incredible Pole Pass. The challenge of this activity is to have the whole group stand in a circle and pass the poles at the same time without dropping them. This activity is done by having each person in the group circle begin by holding a pole vertically so the bottom touches the ground. Poles can start in the right hand. The leader of the group can count to three and the group members release their poles while their neighbor grabs them with their left hand. The pole is then transferred to the right hand and the process repeated. Did I mention that the poles switch poles simultaneously? At the outset, it's trickier than it sounds!

Several passing variations are a fun way to challenge the group. The first is passing to the left direction, the opposite of how you started. A second variation is to skip a person when exchanging the poles. This also can be done in either direction. The third variation is to carefully toss the poles to the person on the right, to the left, or two people away.

As with any of these awesome activities, it's nice to have wrap-up conversation on the activity. Ask questions such as, "Could the group have done anything different to make this activity go more smoothly?" And, "Can you think of a way in which this activity could relate to our everyday lives?"

The Pole Pass was described in a book entitled the New Games Book published in 1976 In this book, the activity is called "Lummisticks."

Squareville

Icebreaker two is called Squareville. This team-building activity works great for large groups. It begins by placing four Nordic poles in a square with their ends touching. The poles need to be the same length. The challenge here is to have the entire group fit inside the square. Karl Rohnke provided a description of this activity in his book, *Silver Bullets*.

Drop squat

Drop squat is the name is the next activity. This game is done best in groups of two. I like Drop Squat because it involves the use of reflexes. After the group is divided into pairs, they face each other. One person holds a pole with both hands from underneath while the partner extends his or her hands above the pole. The person with the hands underneath lets go of the pole. The objective is for the to catch the pole before it hits the ground. The challenge is working together as a team. Make sure you change places. An interesting variation is for the person who catches the pole to catch it with their eyes closed. Only using their sense of touch to catch the pole. *(From LEKI Instructor Training Sessions)*

Pole Juggling

Next up on our hit game list is the Brilliant Pole Juggling. Because of my background in circus theatre, this exercise is one of my personal favorites. Jugglers call this endeavor club passing. This is a partner activity. In groups of two, have the participants face each other using only one pole between them to start. (Please view photo on this page to visualize pole movement.) Here goes — in a clockwise direction, the pole (held vertically in the center) is tossed from the right hand to your partner's right hand. After your partner catches the pole with their mirror hand (left). They toss it to their right then straight across to the partner's left. This sounds much harder than it is. I've had ninety-year-old students can do this one, so you can, too! The pole, when continuously tossed, maintains a rectangular pattern.

When this has been mastered, a second pole can be added to the pattern. Keep them going in the same direction. When you've got the feel for this, you are on your way to the circus. Add three, then four. If your partner is David Copperfield, add about ten more poles and watch them disappear. For a variation on this, go in the opposite direction. *(From LEKI Instructor Training Sessions)*

Pole Balance

I like to call the next activity the Pole Balance. Pretty Creative, huh? Anyhow, I've actually have done this with a peacock feather, and it's kind of fun and kids love it. Using a pole with a rubber tip, place the pole vertically on your index finger straight to the sky. This can also be done on your palm. A fun variation is to balance on your toe. A helpful tip is to focus on the top or other end of the pole. You need to follow where the pole goes.

Pole Relay

The next group activity is the Pole Relay. Divide the group into two lines. The line leader of each group starts with a pole. While each group member is facing forward, the leader passes the pole to the person behind. This is done by twisting the body to the right and handing the vertical pole to the person behind. This continues until the pole goes down the line to the end person. When the pole reaches the final person, the whole group can turn and the end person becomes the line leader. This person passes the poles to their left. Variations on the Pole Relay can be under the legs and over the back. *(From LEKI Instructor Training Sessions)*

Nordic Limbo

A favorite beach party activity is the Limbo. This also works great with the poles in what I call the Nordic Limbo. To start with, have a person on each side of the pole hold it at chest height. The object is to go underneath the pole (leading with the chest) without hitting the pole. This can be done in a line. When everyone has gone under one, lower the pole and so on, until there's only one person left. A variation could be to do the Nordic Limbo blindfolded.

When doing these games and icebreakers, please use caution and be safe. If you come up with any other games with the poles, please let me know (my contact information is in the back of the book).

"My asthma isn't so bothersome since walking with the Nordic poles."

~ Dixie

Chapter Eight

"Teachers open the door,

but you must walk through it yourself."

~ Chinese Proverb

Pole Resistance Partner Exercises for Upper Body

Tip: Communicate with your partner. Let him/her
know if you need more resistance.

These are just a handful of fun exercises that partners can do in
between games and Nordic walking. Credit for these go the talented
trainers at LEKI, a major manufacturer of Nordic equipment. If you
come up with additional fitness activities with the poles please, send
them to me. They may make it into my next Nordic walking book.

Triceps Press Downs

- Partners face each other.
- Feet shoulder width apart.
- Knees bent slightly.
- Person doing the press downs places hands on the inside of pole.
- Overhand grip.
- Partners hands are on the outside in an underhand grip.
- Elbows close to sides at 90 degrees to start.
- Press down as partner provides resistance.
- Switch places after 5-10 repetitions.

(From LEKI Instructor Training Sessions)

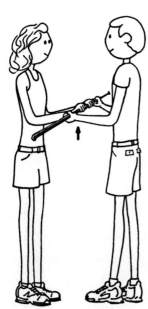

Bicep Curl

- Partners face each other.
- Feet shoulder width apart.
- Knees bent slightly.
- Person doing the curl places hands on the inside of the pole in an underhand grip.
- Partner uses an overhand grip hands outside.
- Elbows to the side at 90 degrees Partner provides resistance to the person doing the curl.
- Switch places after 5-10 repetitions.

(From LEKI Instructor Training Sessions)

Push and Pull Press
Targeting Chest

- Partners face each other.
- One foot forward and one back for your base.
- Forward leg's knee bends as you push.
- Both hands open on pole.
- One person places hands on outside of pole.
- Person on the outside pushes while partner provides resistance.
- Switch roles after 5-10 repetitions.

(From LEKI Instructor Training Sessions)

Above: Vail Colorado,
Left: Vancouver, Canada

"When I Nordic walk with my children
it is a meditative experience. Our
bonding time together, has made us
closer since we started Nordic walking."

~ Lindy

Chapter Nine

"The mind has the same power as the hands:
not merely to grasp the world but to change it."
~ *Colin Wilson*

Let's Walk and Roll

All across America, we hear about overweight kids. I've run into countless numbers of adults who have shared with me their personal stories of when they were young. Most say they had physical education five days per week, walked two miles to school, and played outdoors after school until dark. Summit conferences are taking place on a national level to seek solutions to our societal dilemma. Why are doctors and people who follow trends in the youth culture so concerned about our kids' weight?

Here is what we know for sure: There is a dramatic increase in type 2 diabetes among children. The combination of physical inactivity and poor diet has been a contributing factor. In the past 20 years, the number of children who are obese and have diabetes has increase nationwide by 300%.

Physical inactivity also contributes to chronic conditions such as coronary heart disease, hypertension, colon cancer, and osteoporosis. Forty percent of all elementary schools have cut recess or are in the process of doing so. Overweight children are more likely to become overweight

adults. The recommended amount of moderate or vigorous physical daily activity is 60 minutes. Physicians and experts recommend no more than two hours of TV and computer time per day. Poor diet and physical inactivity lead to 300,000 deaths each year. There is a link with obesity and asthma in girls and young women 9 to 26 years old.

Obesity is on track to surpass tobacco as the top U.S. killer. Alarmingly, obesity is rising fast among preschoolers and is up 10% among this age group. Childhood obesity is linked to depression and self-image.

Let's take a moment to look at the positive things occurring in our society with this crisis. We are starting to see a change in school food service. Salad bars and healthy juices instead of soft drinks are making their way into schools. The new government food pyramid includes an exercise component, and is geared more to the individual. Healthier food choices are being offered at restaurants especially fast food eating establishments.

We need to change our priorities as a society. I would love to see a back-to-basics approach. An example of this is having family dinner be a pleasant and secure experience. It would be nice to create meals and eat together. Family dinner always seemed to be a place for family bonding in our household.

For a fun family weekend, take a bike ride, organize an Olympic day in the neighborhood, or spend some time hiking and walking. There are so many choices for the youth of today that can take their time away from being active. If the whole family is supportive, the children are more likely to join in. The adults in the household are the closest and most important role models, and the children tend to follow their lead.

One of the newer forms of doing a healthy and fun activity is Nordic walking. I personally find this social activity to be exhilarating. Being able to use poles when walking can be a bit tricky to start with. Not only do you have to worry about one foot in front of another, but with the addition of the poles, the coordination problems fly right out the window. After the technique is mastered (which can be done in an hour's time), the activity is fantastic. The children to whom I have taught Nordic walking love the experience. A new twist is added to the age-old activity of walking with the cool Nordic walking poles. The benefits of Nordic walking are many. It's a form of exercise that uses the whole body. Nordic walking allows you to burn 40% more calories than traditional walk-ing. The activity reduces pressure on joints, and increases oxygen consumption 20% to 25%. With education and the help of families and communities, we can get back to a society that sees being active and making healthy eating choices not only a priority, but a regular part of our everyday life.

(*This is a reprint from an article written for the September/October, 2005 Issue of Walk About Magazine, by Tim Arem*).

" Nordic walking has helped me lose weight. I've lost 20 lbs!"

~ Pete

Web Resources

Organizations

1). www.anwa.us
American Nordic Walking Association – An association to belong to for Nordic walking. Features Technique, Equipment, Training & Education, Workshops & Seminars, Research, Health Benefits, & News.
2). www.nordicwalkingusa.com
International Nordic Walking Association – USA Branch Features Health Benefits, Research, Technique, Warming-up, Education, equipment, Testimonials, & Pictures.
3). www.inwa.verkkopolku.com
INWA was founded in Finland in 2000 and focuses on Education and Media
4). www.nordicportal.net
Nordic walking and Fitness Portal

Vancouver, Canada

Media

1). www.walkaboutmag.com
Cool website devoted to all things related to walking. Based in Oregon and sent out bimonthly.
2). www.mountvernonnews.com/local/062204/nordic.walking.html
"Nordic Walking: New Trend in Fitness" by Beth Durbin
3).www.urbanpoling.com/mediamain.php
This site has several media articles you can explore.
4). www.azcentral.com/health/fitness/articles/0226walking-poles.html
Newspaper article on Nordic walking and how walking poles really help.

General Information

1). www.daviddowner.com
Very interesting, friendly site for Nordic walkers. Fascinating site with blogs, events, research, coaching tips, Q &A, moments of inspiration, and recipe of the month.
2). www.intraspec.ca
From Canada, one of the best overall websites with articles, overviews of Nordic walking,

testimonials, technique, equipment, trends, and clinical reference.
3). www.nordicwalker.com
Featuring the Exel pole, benefits of Nordic walking, news, events, retailers, and Exel instructors.
4). www.nordicwalking.co.uk
Site includes information from the UK on poles, classes, news, technique, and benefits.
5). www.nordic walkingonline.com
Simple, yet great source for learning what Nordic walking is.
6). www.nordicwalkingus.com
An informative community site from on of the pioneers of Nordic walking in the US. Focus is on poles, beginning Nordic walking, and weekly articles.
7). www.urbanpoling.com
Canadian site with focus on products, research, technique, testimonials, events, and newsletters.

History

1). www.chicagotribune.com/news/local/chi_,0602280139feb28.1, 2641846.story
Research studies on how we learned to walk like a man, by William Mullen.
2). www.exerstrider.com
Tom Rutlin's contribution.
3). www.inwa.verkkopolku.com
4). www.nordicwalking online.com

Technique

1). www.cbsnews.com/stories/2006/01/20/earlyshow/health/main1224797.shtml

Nordic Walking Catching On.
2). www.daviddowner.com/archive/ed3/tips.html
Tips: Straps are important
3). www.fittrek.com
NW Techniques – How to
4). www.intraspec.ca/nordic-walking.php
5). www.nordicwalking.com
6). www.nordicwalking online.com
Basic technique, Instructional DVD/VHS/e-book
7). www.nordicwalkingus.com
Straight arm or bent arm technique?
8). www.nordicwalkingusa.com
Techniques for beginners and basic technique
9). www.urbanpoling.com/technique.php
The Exerstrider poles technique

Benefits

1). www.fittrek.com
Benefits for weight loss, fitness, fitness clubs, power walkers, hikers/backpackers, runners, knee or hyper habilitation, pre/post natal.
2). www.irule.co.nz
New Zealand website, iRULE
3). www.leki.com
4). www.nordicwalking online.com
5). www.nordicwalking.com
Health Facts
6) www.nordicwalkingusa.com/benefits.htm
www.nordicwalkingusa.com/research.htm
Health facts

7) www.womens-menopause-health.com/exercise/nordic_walking.htm *Women's Menopause Health Center*

Nordic walking Research Articles

1). Scientific Evidence on Nordic walking nordicwalking.net.nz/index.aspx?pageID=8

2). Acute responses to using walking poles in patients with coronary artery disease.
Walter P.R., Porcari J.P., Brice G., Terry L.
Journal of Cardiopulmonary Rehabilitation, 1996 Jul – Aug; 16 (4):245-50

3). Effects of walking poles on lower extremity gait mechanics. Wilson J., Torry M.R., Decker M.J., Kernozek T., Steadman J.R. Medicine and Science in Sports and Exercise, Vol.33, No.1, 2001, pp.142-147

4). Efficiency of walking and stepping: relationship to body fatness. Chen K.Y., Acra S.A., Donahue C.L., Sun M., Buchowski M.S. Obesity research, 2004 Jun;12 (6):982-9

5). Research on the benefits of Nordic walking. Research summary compiled by Raija Laukkanen, Ph.D., Docent Director, Exercise Science, Polar electro Oy, Finalnd. This (2001) summary is presented on many Nordic walking site. See also PMC Paramedisch Centrum Roosendaal. Fysiotherapie e.d.

for additional references.

6). Effects of a walking program on attribual style, depression, and self esteem in women. Palmer L.K. Perceptual and Motor Skills, 1995 Dec, 81 (3 pt1):891-8.

Articles 2-6 were taken from www.intraspec.ca/nordic-walking.php

Testimonials

1) www.daviddowner.com
2) www.fittrek.com
3) www.nordicwalkingusa.com

Equipment
Poles

1) www.exerstrider.com
2) www.fittrek.com
3) www.keytz.com
4) www.komperdell.com
5) www.leki.com
www.walkingsmarter.com
LEKI poles, Children size poles available.
6) www.nordiccomposite.com
Western Pole Company, INC. Nordic Composite Poles
7) www.nordicwalking.com
www.nordicwalkingusa.com
www.exelsports.net
Exel Poles
8) ww.nordicwalkingus.com
www.skiwalking.com
www.swixsport.com
Swix Poles
9) www.netando.de
Axess Nordic walking Poles
10) www.sport-tiedje.de.com
An European online Catalog. Abby, Fischer, Fizan and One Way brands.

Socks

1) www.defeet.com
DeFeet Socks
2) www.foxsox.com
Fox River Mills
3) www.linmfg.com
Lin Socks
4) www.newbalancesocks.com
New balance
5) www.smartwool.com
Smart Wool
6) www.thorlosocks.com
www.extremesocks.com
Thorlos
7) www.wigwam.com
Wigwam Mills
8) www.wrightsock.com
Wright Socks
9). www.injinji.com
Injinji Socks

Walking Shoes

1) www.adidasus.com
Adidas
2) www.birkenstockusa.com
BIRKENSTOCK
3) www.clarkshoes.com
Clarks
4) www.columbia.com
Columbia
5) www.easyspirit.com
Easy Spirit
6) www.ecco.com
Ecco
7) www.lowaboots.com
LOWA
8) www.montrail.com
Montrail
9) www.reebok.com
Reebok
10) www.rockport.com
ROCKPORT

11) www.salomonsports.com
SALOMON
12) www.saucony.com
SAUCONY
13) www.timberland.com
Timberland
14) www.vasque.com
VASQUE

Emergency Identification Shoelaces

www.idonme.com
www.roadid.com

Shoelace System

www.yanks.com

Arch Supports and Insoles

www.archcrafters.com
www.footsmart.com
www.footshax.com
www.spenco.com
www.sorbothane.com
www.powersteps.com
www.drscholls.com
www.superfeet.com
www.shockdoc.com
www.birkenstock.com
www.shockblockers.com
www.walkfit.com (a very creative website)

Foot Powder

www.Neatfeat.net - *Neat Feat*
www.drscholls.com - *Dr. Scholls*
www.goldbond.com - *Gold Bond*
www.chandlerssoaps.com
Chandlers Soaps

Sunscreens

www.bananaboat.com
www.coppertone.com
www.jason-natural.com
www.murad.com
www.neutrogena.com

Sunglasses

www.bolle.com
www.oakley.com
www.rayban.com
www.smithsport.com
www.thenorthface.com

Water Carrier

www.amphpod.com
www.aquaclip.com
www.camelbak.com
www.fuelbelt.com
www.hydrapak.com
www.leki.com
www.orgear.com
www.outdoorproducts.com
www.polarusa.com
www.sigonline.com
www.ultimatedirection.com
www.waterbelt.com

Sport Drinks

www.gusports.com - *GU*
www.gatorade.com - *Gatorade*
www.uspowerade.com
Powerade

www.eas.com - *EAS*
www.ultimatereplenisher.com
Ultima
www.frsplus.com - *FRS Plus*
www.cytosport.com
Cytosport
www.endura.com - *Endura*
www.accelerade.com
Accelerade

Energy Bars

www.balance.com
Balance Gold
www.clifbar.com - *Clif Bars*

www.powerbar.com
PowerBar Harvest,
Whole Grain Energy Bars
www.honeystinger.com
Honey Stinger Energy Bars
www.purefit.com
Purfit Nutrition Bars

www.odwalla.com - *Odwalla*
www.philsbar.com - *Phils' Bar*
www.revivalsoy.com
Revival Soy
www.livingfuel.com
Living Fuel
www.kashi.com
Kashi Energy Bars

Energy Gels

www.gusports.com
GU Energy Gel
www.carbboom.com
Carb-Boom Energy Gel
www.powerbar.com
Power Gel
www.clifbar.com
Clif Shot Energy Gel

www.honeystinger.com
*Honey Stinger Natural
Energy Gel*

Training

1) www.nordicwalkingonline.com
Instructional DVD/VHS/e-book
2) www.terrischneider.net
Training by use of the Internet
3) www.activeusa.com
*Visual trainer, Nordic walking
community, and message board.*

Fun Equipment

1). www.nordictrekkers.com
*Nordic Trekkers Fitness and
Strength by Volaris USA, Inc.*

Trek Torpedo: Radically unique poles
with 1-liter water chambers at the
bottom, add as much or as little
resistance as you want.

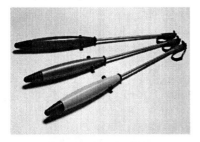

2). www.more4nordic.de/nordic/
indoor_frame.htm
*Check out this unique site from
Germany.* Turn the music up and
groove.
3). www.nordicbalance.de/
NordicInlineSkating/tabid/
82/default. aspx
4) www.zfit.com
*Nordic Blading, Nordic Blading
Poles. Exel and Leki*

Travel Resorts that Offer Nordic walking

1) www.gofinland.org/web/
us/publish.nsf
*Site from Finland where the activ-
ity started. Focus on publication
from Finnish Tourist Board
Focus on travel in Finland.*
2) www.biltmore.com
*Biltmore estate, Asheville, North
Carolina. Located on 8,000 acres,
experience Biltmore's beauty
through the Outdoor Center.
Explore gardens and woodland
trails.*

*Biltmore Estate and the Inn on
Biltmore, Asheville, NC*

3). www.beavercreek.snow.com
*Beaver Creek Resort, Vail,
Colorado is an awesome resort
that offers classes in Nordic
walking.*
4). www.crystalmountain.com
*Crystal Mountain Resort in
Thompsonville, MI. The 1st resort
to offer Nordic walking in the US.
They are consistently rated the #1
ski resort in the Midwest.
Excellent customer service and
perfect for families.*
5). www.garlandusa.com
*Garland Resort in Lewiston, MI.
It has the largest log structure*

east of the Mississippi. Only 4
star Golf Resort in Michigan.
6). www.homesteadresort.com
*The Homestead Resort in Glen
Arbor, MI. Americas Fresh Water
Resort with a mile of sandy beach
located in Sleeping Bear Dunes
National Lakeshore.*
7). www.timberridgeresort.com
*Timber Ridge Resort and RV Park
in Traverse City, MI*

Warm up and cool-down

1). www.active.com
*Active women fit facts: a great
stretch, reasons to warm up, and
how to build muscle. An article.*
2). www.fischer-ski.com
*Nordic walking bring on the
Young*
3). www.gotakanal.se
*Nordic walking School part 2,
Warm Up.*
4). www.inwa.verkkopolku.com
*Warm up and cool down exercises
with descriptions and
illustrations.*
5). www.leki.com
*Easy to follow warming up
exercises.*
6). www.nordicwalkingusa.com
*Nine warm up exercises with
photos*
7). www.polewalk.com
*Remember warm up and cool
down. This site shows you how to
do warm up and cool down exercises with photos.*
8). www.swixsport.com
*Great site to learn about how to
warm up and stretch out. It had
descriptions and illustrations.*

Heart Rate Monitors

www.polarusa.com
www.bodytronics.com
www.highgear.com

Pedometers

www.highgear.com
www.omron.com
www.bodytronics.comBio

Hey, where can I find this book?

Good Question!

Order online at

www.booksurge.com

or at

www.TboneRun.com

Glossary

Nordic walking – fitness walking with specifically designed poles.

Adjustable Pole – a pole that can be adjusted in size (it may have one or more adjustments).

Non-adjustable Pole – pole that only has one size and no adjustments.

Trigger – a quick-release system used with the straps.

Rubber Tip – cover for the end of the pole for use on pavement or indoors.

Grip – area where you place your hand, once through the strap.

Shaft – generally made from metal, the main part of the pole.

Strap – used to engage the hand to the pole in a comfortable fashion.

Pole – long circular tube used for Nordic walking.

Stick – not used in Nordic walking. (Tell a Nordic Walker you use a stick instead of a pole and they may impale you with their pole.)

Basket – used at the end of the pole to prevent the pole from sinking in snow or soft ground.

Nordic Inline Skating – Inline skating with Nordic poles.

Hip Pack – used to carry goodies (water and snacks) around the hip while Nordic walking. No you don't have to be hip to own one.

Favorite places to Nordic Walk...

Notes...

1305650

Made in the USA